How to Become a 3D Printing Entrepreneur

By Yoni Binstock

Table of Content

About the Author

Introduction

A new technology is emerging and is poised to transform our world in unimaginable ways. As former Editor in Chief of Wired Magazine and author of "Makers: The New Industrial Revolution" Mark Anderson put it about 3D printing "It will be bigger than the Web".

Put yourself in the shoes of the early innovators working on the personal computer in the 1980s. No one believed that they would be in every household, and thought they were only useful for big corporations like IBM. But entrepreneurs, like Bill Gates and Steve Jobs, saw the computer's potential and only a few years later, billions of people now have one and the technology has radically shaped our society and world.

I believe 3D printing is on that precipice. The technology has historically been isolated in universities and research labs, but is now being used in a wide range of different industries and is quickly changing the way in which we make real world products.

3D printing is being utilized today solving real-world problems, prototyping new designs, and create beautiful artwork. Welcome to the exciting and ever-changing world of 3D printing!

About the Book

This book is for anyone that is interested in becoming a 3D printing entrepreneur. With the information from this book, you'll have a great view into the world of 3D printing and be able to build a business using this amazing technology. We'll first (briefly) focus on the technology and the differences that set it apart from normal manufacturing. The second chapter will focus on designers and engineers and how they can use their skills to generate revenue. In the third chapter, we'll focus on those who want to purchase a printer, the different types, and how you can make (and save) money. The fourth chapter will cover ancillary niches, including software, materials, and printer parts. In the last chapter, you'll hear from amazing 3D printing entrepreneurs about the path they took and their suggestions for you to build a successful business. At the end of the book, we've researched and listed over 50 resources to help you on your way in becoming a 3D printing entrepreneur.

What is 3D Printing?

Also known as additive manufacturing, 3D printing is a new manufacturing method, vastly different from the normal subtractive method that creates most of the physical goods we interact day to day with. The traditional method used since the industrial revolution is based on the premise of taking a slab of a raw material (plastic, wood, metal, clay) and removing parts of it to reveal the end model.

As the name implies, in 3D printing, the object is instead "printed" by a multi-dimensional processes adding layers upon layers, which are placed on top of one another to form a 3D object.

The first step in 3D printing is generating a CAD image (more in the following chapter). The CAD file is then converted to an STL file, which the 3D printer can read. With the information, the printer can start printing and know exactly where to place material on the x, y, and z-axis.

There are two main types of 3D printing which are readily used today including selective laser sintering (SLS) and fused deposition modeling (FDM). There are also a few other methods including stereolithography (SLA), selective laser melting (SLM), direct metal laser sintering (DMLS), laminated object manufacturing (LOM), and fused deposition modeling (FDM).

Create it REAL

How 3D Printing is Used Today

3D printing was first patented in 1986, but was largely isolated to universities. Just in the past decade, the price of the technology has fallen so quickly that it is now being used around the world by hobbyist to the biggest multi-national corporations. Currently, 3D printing is being utilized to create clothing, eyewear, prototypes, jewelry, buildings, food, artwork, medical devices, toys, human organs, and much more! 3D printing is still in its early stages of development, but has already been transformative in many industries.

Where 3D Printing Thrives

Complex/technical objects: Regular manufacturing often can't be precise or create intricate objects. There are many ways artists and designers can fill the gaps in artwork and product design where regular manufacturing lags. It is always useful to remember that with 3D printing, complexity is free.

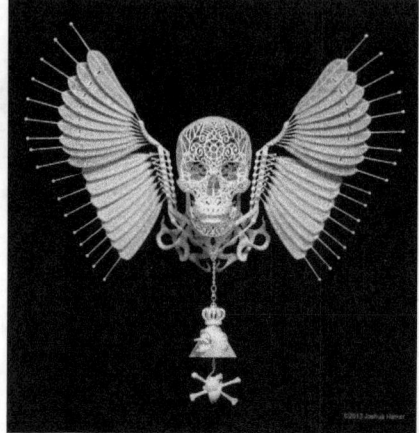

Anatomica di Revolutis by Josh Harker.

Artwork: 3D printing offers an entirely new medium for artists who enjoy working in three dimensions. With new materials and technologies, the precision, range of colors, and textures, the diversity of artwork keeps on growing.

Eric van Straaten's 3D-printed sculptures.

Fashion: In a somewhat unusual circumstance, the fashion world is adopting this new technology faster than many other industries. The ability to create custom and small batches is perfect in designing the next pair of shoes or a runway dress.

Sebastian Errazuriz's 12 Shoes for 12 Lovers.

Functional objects: While many of the most popular items sold on 3D printing stores have been artwork other great sellers are functional tools to enhance some one's life. Think about the devices we work with throughout the day and how 3D printing may add value to it.

Infinite Sisu iPad stand.

Jewelry: For similar reasons as fashion, jewelry is a great niche to focus on for 3D printing. It is often one of the top sellers on websites like Shapeways and a great way to get into the industry with small, low cost items.

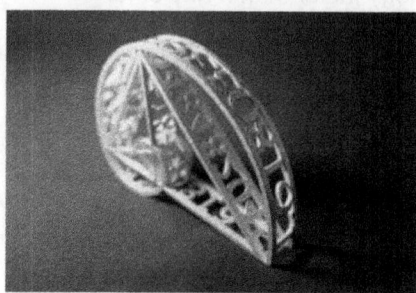

Ashley Zelinskie's code and art.

In large manufacturing like the car and aerospace industry, companies are able to significantly lower their R&D cost by cheaply and quickly print many different prototypes. This is a great way to start your 3D printing business. Offer either your design expertise or your 3D printer as a way for engineers, architects, industrial designers, artists, and other creative types the ability to hold their idea in their hand for a marginal fee. One of the main highlights of 3D printing is the small production cost to test an idea and to iterate on new ones.

Another advantage of 3D printing is the ability to easily customize each new model. In regular manufacturing, a whole line needs to be refitted costing tens of thousands of dollars to make the smallest adjustment. With 3D printing, you can have a template model, let's say a prosthetic hand and to make it a custom fit for each buyer requires only a few adjustments on the design and not a single added penny in the production cost. Imagine ways where you could have a model that people would want to purchase a customized version for themselves.

There are a few business principles that apply specifically to the 3D printing industry that you should know.

One, you should focus on the strengths of 3D printing. Aim to sell objects that are low in volume, can fit in print area of a printer, incorporate complexity or personalization, and are light (for cheaper shipping).

Two, concentrate on a niche market. Like any other businesses, the more defined your target market it, the better you can focus on it. It can be dice for Dungeons & Dragons, Zelda themed jewelry, or objects for any other cohort.

Three, you will never be able to compete on price with mass produced goods. Your goal should be to sell models that are between $50-$200 and have at least a 30% profit margin. If you're selling more a hundred copies of your models every month, consider raising your price.

Four, understand the average buyer of 3D printed models. Because the technology is still new, the average American isn't buying products made with 3D printing. Find the people who are and understand their passions and hobbies because those are the only ones that will buy from you in the immediate future.

Five, a main priority should be providing your prospective buyers with novelty. Your item must clearly demonstrate that it could not have been made by regular manufacturing and the buyer is buying it so that he/she can show that they are an early adopter.

For Designers

Skills Needed

While creating objects with 3D printer might seem like something from Star Trek (which it is), the reality is that many already are doing it today and you can, with dedicated focus, learn how to turn your ideas into reality. But, while there are great online tools to help you learn any number of the following software tools, it will not come easy, and be prepared to spend considerable amount of time learning if this is the route you want to take.

There are a many 3D software packages available today for 3D printing designers. Here are my top picks.

For beginners, I recommend one of the following: Google SketchUp, Autodesk 123D, and TinkerCaD. My personal favorite is Google SketchUp since it's free as well as being particularly easy to learn and use. TinkerCad is also extremely easy to use, and for individuals without any design training, this is great software to start with.

Software that are a little more advance and especially targeted for more artistic people, here are the software tools that are most popular: Zbrush, Sculptris, and Mudbox.

Those who are geared towards programming, the best 3D modeling software to use are: OpenSCAD, ModelBuilder, and Grasshopper.

Lastly, for the most advanced 3D printing designer, the best software tools are Blender, 3ds Max, Maya, Rhino, and Modo. Having a grasp of any of these top software programs will enable you to charge a premium on your services. The range and complexity of models you will be able to produce will be extensive, but keep in mind the steep learning curve.

If you're new to the field, I would recommend starting with Google SketchUp and once getting the basic building blocks down before moving up to more advanced software.

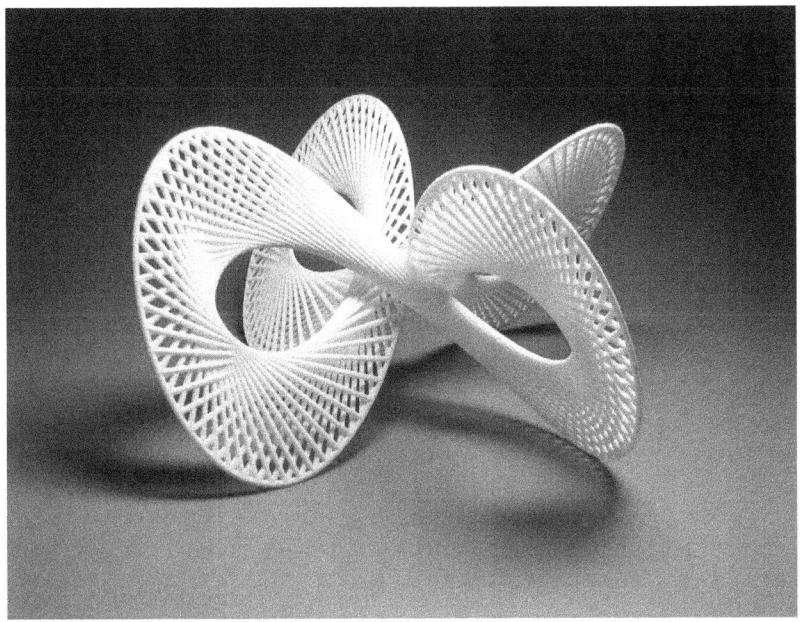

Freelancing vs 9-5

There are many different options for 3D designers to turn their skills into cash. One way is through freelancing. Sites such as Odesk, Elance, and Freelancer are perfect to find people to hire you for short projects. Being a freelancer has tons of great benefits, especially choosing how your spend your time, but be honest with yourself on the prices you can charge, how many clients you expect to close, and how many projects you can work at the same time.

I would recommend sticking with only one of the above websites. One of the decisive attributes a client is looking for is a portfolio and work history. If you're getting jobs all over the place, it may not be as advantageous to you then having a large list of clients on one platform.

Another way to bring in the 3D printing dough is to design your own models and sell them through stores like Shapeways (you can find others in the resources section). The advantage of this method is that you have full creative freedom and choose what you get to work on. The disadvantage of this method is that have to market your store and products. Although you may have the next best thing, you need the world to see it. If you're lacking online marketing expertise, you might consider designing models for other people and companies for the immediate future.

Here are 10 pointers about selling your own models.

One, have your models in as many locations as possible. Use eBay, Etsy, Shapeways, iMaterialize, Pinshape, Threeding, and any other site to get your models in front of as many eye balls as possible.

Two, experiment with changing your pricing. Try to sell a few of your models with as small margin as possible and once it has a few sales, later increasing the price.

Three, use competitions, social media, and forums to get to your models shown to the people who work at the platforms where your models are being hosted. A sure way to get sales is to be listed as a staff favorite or featured pick.

Four, although not necessary (and something I don't do myself), try to have a theme throughout your models and store. Make it easy for a customer to purchase more than one model from your store.

Five, consider offer products in a range of prices. Customers, in many cases, will pick the models in the middle so use more expensive and cheaper products to "frame" the main ones you want to sell.

Six, use your own social media channels. Be proud of what you create and share it with friends, family, and the world. You never know if a high school friend might really like what you're creating.

Seven, see what the models are selling on the marketplace that your using. Although, you may find a niche that has enough customers, keep your mind on what type of objects are sold most.

Eight, invest in a graphic designer to design a store logo. For $5 on Fiverr or $99 on 99 Designs, you can get a well done design for your store. If you have a poorly made banner, you will lose customers.

Nine, write compelling content on your store page and under your products. Don't waste weeks or months designing a beautiful model only to ruin your sales with poor grammar. Spend the time working on revisions or hire someone else to do it for you.

Ten, prepare to hustle. As I mentioned, just because you designed a model doesn't mean you'll be rolling in money like Scrooge McDuck. You should assume that every person that will buy your model will have to be driven by you. There are lots of great resources on online marketing, but make sure that you don't get inundated by them. Learn quickly and just do it.

For 3D designers who prefer to work at a company, there are many opportunities available for them as well. According to the site Glassdoor, 3D designers start out with a projected income of $52,000 a year. A great advantage of being a 3D designer is that there are many ways to use your skills to crossover to other industries like animation, gaming, and engineering and you shouldn't have an issue landing a well-paying job. Although this book is targeted towards entrepreneurs, a great way to build a portfolio and grow your skill set is to work for a company as a designer for a few months or a year.

3D Printer Owner

When it comes to 3D printers, there are many high quality printers available for "professionals" and there are many that have a lower cost and are perfect for amateurs. The following is a list of the highest rated 3D printers, starting with the Printrbot Simple Maker. Other highly rated printers include the MakerGeeks RepRap Mini

Kossel which is rated as the best DIY 3D printer, the Cubify Cube 3 which is rated as the best 3D printer for beginners, the Hyrel E2 Hobbyist which is rated as the best 3D printer for experimenters, and the Stratasys Mojo which is rated as the best 3D printer for small businesses. The specific printer that you choose should reflect your particular needs and desires. See the resources page at the end of the book for a more extensive list of different printers.

*Note: New 3D printers are coming out every month and without a doubt this list will be outdated within the year (2014).

Connect Your Printer to the World

Let's say you have a printer – awesome! As soon as you get in the mail, you're going to be having the printer up and running that day and will have models flying off the deck. But, after a while, you'll run out of stuff to print. Luckily, you can use services like MakeXYZ and add your printer to an online pool and people geographically around you can pay you to print something for them. It's a great way to earn some cash when your printer would be instead sitting idle. Similar services include CowFab, 3D Hubs, Azavy, and you3Dit.

Save Money

A great part of owning a 3D printer is that there are thousands of objects you can print rather than purchasing them from a store. Owning a 3D printer can save an average household thousands of dollars on everyday household items. Items such as shower heads, shoe insoles, coffee mugs, spare parts, toys, etc. can all be created through a 3D printer. Researchers at the Michigan Technological University conducted a study to find out how much a family might save by printing common objects. They found that the savings came out to between $294 and $1,926, depending on the quality of the comparable retail products. Not many people talk about saving money with a 3D printer, but there's not any difference between saving and earning the same amount of money. It's cash in the bank. Make a list of items that you regularly buy and see if they can be 3D printed – perhaps you can save thousands as well.

Ancillary

While many of you will either use your design skills or a physical 3D printer, it's good to learn about all the other possible ways to build a business with 3D printing. In the computer industry, the hardware people were the main drivers of innovation for the first two decades. But, new companies like Facebook, PayPal, Amazon, and Google were soon built on top of the existing technology to create a new group of internet billionaires. What will be the game changer company for 3D printing? Will you be the one who comes up with the idea?

Copyright and Privacy

An interesting and possibly volatile part of 3D printing has to do with copyright. Many large firms will seek protection of their intellectual property as it becomes easy to scan, upload, share, and print their products around the world. Companies like Secured 3D are able to protect 3D models by deleting the file as soon as it's printed. As many of the readers will remember back in the 2000s, there were host of issues with copyright infringement over music that was shared and downloaded via the internet. The same issues are liable to occur again with 3D printing and there will be lots of opportunities for innovators who seek to secure IP for companies and for others who want to find ways around it.

3D Printing Materials

Another option to take is to sell 3D printed materials. Not all 3D printers create items from the same types of materials and many 3D printers have very specific materials that they can create objects with. Some popular 3D printing materials include plastic resin, composite filament, wood fill pellets, ceramic filled polymers, recycled plastic, bronze and bamboo fill, nylon filament, metal, and others. If this is a field that interests you, look for ways to acquire one or two material in large quantities and sell it a profit to individual users.

Scanning

3D scanning is a very cool technology that fits very well with 3D printing. 3D scanning allows you to scan an object and then re-create it on your computer. The technology enables you to capture hundred thousand or millions of data points on a physical object to generate very precise images. There are several 3D scanners on the market and you can find many of the top ones in our resources section at the end of the book.

Imagine how you might scan someone's dog and be able to 3D print a representation of it. Many museums are getting behind this technology and scanning their sculptures and models, so if they were ever stolen or broken, they wouldn't be lost to antiquity. Try to find ways to use 3D scanning to digitally capture and protect what's most precious to people and you'll be on your way to riches. This is one of my favorite fields and is filled with many possibilities for a 3D printing entrepreneur.

Teaching

Another great way to make money through 3D printing is by teaching it to others. Since 3D printing is still such a new technology and field, there are very few "experts" in the industry. If you can build a niche and established yourself as a credible expert, you may find opportunities for teaching at schools, consulting business, or creating your own online classes.

Academic fields that are particularly going to be interested in 3D printing will be; engineering, architecture, art, and science. If you have a printer and can bring it into a classroom, it would be possible to print molecules for chemistry students, molds for a cooking class, artifacts for history students, and many other scenarios. It's a great way to keep kids engaged and teach them about an upcoming technology that is sure to be important as they grow older. As many of us took computer classes in elementary and middle school, 3D printing could be very similar and there's currently a large gap between the demand of knowledge and qualified teachers.

Conclusion

"The end of the 20th century was about information becoming digital. The 21st century is going to be about bringing the virtual world into closer alignment with the physical one." Hod Lipson and Melba Kurman in <u>Fabricated: The New World of 3D Printing</u>

3D printing is a great way to make money using the most advanced technology. Businesses can be made with your design skills, a 3D printer, or any number of other opportunities. 3D printing puts the power of creation in the hands of individuals who are interested in making money, creating objects, and making a name for themselves with unique and interesting technology.

The technology is projected to exponentially in the next decade as more and more people are coming to terms with the idea that they too can create objects with their own specifications and even in their own homes. What I especially love about the technology is that it enables all of us to be creators of our physical world. Individuals can use their creativity and imagination to enrich the world through art, engineering, and innovative concepts. Just think of all the new products that are yet to be created with 3D printing!

Don't let this be another book that you just consume and forget a few days later. Write down exactly what you're going to do to move forward in becoming a 3D printing entrepreneur. This is an exciting time to be alive and 3D printing is at the cusp of radically changing our world.

Join the movement and become a 3D printing entrepreneur right now!

From the Experts

I had the privilege of talking with 3D printing entrepreneurs who have been kind enough to share their wisdom with me and with you. They are artists, entrepreneurs, CEOs of multi-million dollar companies, and thought leaders in the field. I asked them how they got into the industry, how my readers can build a 3D printing business, and any other words of insight. Here are their responses.

Andreas – Owner of Woody's Minifig Customs in 3D

I started 3d printing more than 5 years ago as simple solution on the question to how to replace a LEGO that was no longer available, at an acceptable price range, without the need to invest thousands of dollars, and available to everyone in the world without building up a logistic supply chain.

3d printing was the answer. It wasn't that easy at that time, since it took several months to get the first result. But, now I'm able to have my product in hand in just a few days.

I see 3D printing entering our lives in a similar way as the laptop. I expect that there will be a household version in an acceptable quality and price within 3-5 years and an availability of a lot more materials covering more disciplines of business (cars, medicine, fancy stuff, hobby, replacement parts).

The people making the most money in the industry will be 3D printing companies, engineering/design departments, and other institutions. I recommend people who want to become 3D printing entrepreneurs realize that most customers don't care that it's 3D printed, but it's very advantageous for business owners as they can have a small scale production cost.

Bathsheba Grossman – 3D printing artist

I love 3D printing because it can make shapes that traditional sculpture technology either can't do or can only do at prohibitive expense. 3D printing solved a real problem for me because I wanted to make models that could only have been made with a 3D printer.

In the next 5-10 years I'm guessing that the underlying manufacturing environment -- the different machines, processes, and the companies that develop and produce them -- will consolidate rather than diverge further.

I think the flowering of new designers, products, and markets will continue - perhaps a little less breathlessly than in the last few years, but with force and in numbers. As part of that, I also see postprocessing -- integration of 3D printing techniques with preexisting and newly designed casting, finishing, and fabrication methods -- continuing to grow.

I would recommend to budding 3D printing entrepreneurs to make the product first. Before the business plan, before the Kickstarter, before the website. Make sure people want the product. If you show it to them and they say it's nice but their wallet stays in their pocket, they don't want it. Literally you want to see people reach for their wallet at the sight of your product. If you don't have that, well, maybe you're enough of a genius marketer to have a business anyway, but it won't be nearly as much fun.

The changing market conditions are going to continue to be challenging to micro-businesses like mine, as 3D printing has gone from a niche technology to the huge ecosystem we now see. But it is still the perfect medium for the kind of sculptures that I make, and I hope to continue my artistic odyssey with it as long as I live.

Espen Sivertsen – CEO of Type A Machines

I am passionate about 3D printing because it can empower anyone to make anything. If you sat on the bus 10 years ago and had a question, how would you get an answer? Today, thanks to smart phones and Google, 1 billion questions are answered every day. In a similar line, if you are on the bus today and you have an idea, how can you make it real? Well - 3D printing. It's not easy just yet, but it is in fact possible to sit on the bus, model something out on your smart phone, and have it printed before you arrive home. Just think where we might be 10 years from now!

There are four areas the technology will improve on: print quality, print speed, ease of use and reliability. In terms of usage, I think we will see an extension of the first desktop wave towards enthusiasts and professionals, followed by adoption from manufacturers, before finally we get the mass market, print at home desktop 3D printer (but that's years out still).

A great place to start learning about 3D Printing is Reddit's 3D printing forum. They have a great FAQ there: http://www.reddit.com/r/3Dprinting/wiki/index

As technology leaders in the 3D printing industry I feel that we have a shared responsibility particularly towards education and the environment. 3D printing stands to be a great tool, but we need to make sure that it empowers as many people as possible, without adding a further burden to the environment.

Jesse Harrington Au - Chief Maker Advocate at Autodesk

3D Printing offers a world where my ideas can manifest themselves into reality, right before my eyes. It is not limited to my skill set or capabilities. I have always been an advocate of democratizing design, and additive manufacturing allows for this to happen for people anywhere that have access to a computer. Think about the possibilities if everyone had a say in what is created. As a collective brain, we can come up with better solutions than relying on large companies or being limited to purchasing something whose design was dictated by manufacturing price and not quality.

The future of 3D printing will focus on accessibility and material science. Once we break out of our current material and scale limitations, we will be able to design and print nearly anything. I believe an upcoming trend will be in flexible and conductive materials, but, by far, one of the most interesting things happening are the people working on CNC Looms. Can you imagine being able to produce clothing or stretchable inflatable things?

Start today and be sure to spread yourself a bit. There are lots of online stores to sell your wares. If you are thinking about other avenues, I would highly suggest hanging out at maker spaces like TechShop and attending industry shows like 3D Printshow where you can talk to and learn from the leaders in the industry. The market is growing quickly and what it looks like today may not be what it will look like in a year. There are lots of large companies throwing their hat into the ring and that should open up the marketplace for more accessories, 3D printing farms and service options.

It's important to think about additive manufacturing as a new tool, one that touches every industry in the same way that injection molding has for the past 60 years. The difference being is that now, everything can be customized and created in small runs. So consider the industries that have not yet adapted to this and explore if they could benefit from the ability to customize.

Lance Pickens – Co-Founder of Made Solid

Fundamentally, 3D printing is about turning ideas into physical things, I'm fascinated by the thought of being able to hold in my hands those thoughts and ideas. What got me started down this road was the notion that I ought to be able to be on my computer, looking at 3D model, reach into the screen and grab the object.

3D printing is heading everywhere. We've begun to see industry and domain specific machines, and that trend will continue. On the consumer front I believe we will begin to see Photopolymer based 3D printing technology supplant FDM in a long steady shift towards higher fidelity printing. You should also expect convergence between bio-printing and 3D printing and that many 3D printers will offer integrated scanning & printing.

I would recommend visiting your local hacker space and trying the technology for yourself. Another very helpful resource is MAKE magazine; they often publish relevant and useful content.

Lastly, don't give up. Don't listen to the naysayers. Learn about the frustrations people have with 3D printing, and figure out a way to remove that frustration. Solve the hard problems. We've only just begun, our best work lays ahead.

Liza Wallach Kloski and Nick Kloski – Cofounders of <u>HoneyPoint3D</u> <u>Stores</u>

Nick and I started HoneyPoint3D because we believe that everyone is creative with the right tools. 3D Printing allows people that normally don't have access to create models and prototypes without having to go through traditional manufacturing channel that are both expensive and time consuming.

I'm part of the school of thought that believes that most people will have access to a 3D printer in their home or through a service in the years to come. That might be 5 years away, sooner or later, but the point is that regular consumer will learn the value and learn the tools of creation making it as useful as other tools you have in your garage, i.e., a hammer, wrench, etc!

To learn more about 3D printing there are many excellent resources online like LinkedIn groups, 3ders.org and more. Amazon has a good selection of books as well.

Many people are entering the market and it's helpful to know whether you want to be on the hardware side, software side or service side. Everyone should at least spend some time "hands-on" with a 3D printer.

We want people to understand the reality of 3D Printing and where it's at now. We know there is a lot of hype for the industry and it's truly very exciting but also consumers should understand its current limitations. With FDM printed parts you might see tiny lines, the cost may be higher than the same plastic shape you can find at a hardware store and the printing process can be slow. All this is improving but it will take time. Even still, it's a pretty amazing technology and quality improves exponentially.

Mark Hatch – Co-Founder and CEO of TechShop

3D printing, though 30 years old, is an entirely new way of making something. As such, there are plenty of novel things that can't be made any other way. Also, the hype surrounding the new interest in 3D printing is exciting an entire generation of people to get into making things. This will have positive results as new inventions, ideas, products and services are created to leverage this new capability.

I love the cheap printers as they are showing up in classrooms, on peoples desks and in people's homes... like mine. I believe a significant percentage of homes will have a cheap one (sub $400) within the decade. I'm not sure how actually useful they will be, but they will be fun to play with and will occasionally be useful.

My favorite place to learn about 3D printing is at Maker Faires. It was only three or four years ago that we brought one of the first ones to a Maker Faire and by the next year three 3D printer companies were coming to the fair.

You need to go into business to serve a real need, not just because you think the technology is cool. To quote Peter Drucker. "What business are you in?" "Who is your customer?" "What does your customer think is value?" These are usually very difficult questions to answer.

3D printing is one of the ways that computers are making it easier for the amateur to participate in manufacturing. The entire CNC (computer numerically controlled) world is radically changing the other ways of making things. Add in the robotic revolution and we are rapidly entering a new industrial revolution where anyone with a good idea will be able to build that idea cheaply.

Patrick Durgin-Bruce – Co-Founder and Creative Director of Mymo

One of the biggest opportunities with 3D printing is the ability to produce customizable products that are specifically tailored and produced for the end user. After the industrial revolution, we've had a century of manufacturing and design centered around mass production. But with 3D printing and other digital technologies, we are starting to have the ability to design products that are based not on a singular design with just a few options for color or size, but to truly personalize the end product. The challenge is to get product designers to think not in terms of a singular design, but to create products around a design system that allows for flexibility and personalization.

As a graphic designer, I was not formally trained in dimensional art, or 3D printing at all. I was able to teach myself 3D modeling software from tutorials and videos online, and learn the techniques and limitations of the technology from articles online. Just dive in with a project, and learn what you need to get it done as you go.

The key to building a successful business is to look at it from the customer's point of view. The challenge is not "What can we do with 3D printing?" but rather, "What problem can we solve that will make people's lives better?" Ask yourself why your product is being 3D printed. What are you offering the customer that couldn't be done, or couldn't be done as easily, through conventional product manufacturing?

Relative to the history of product design, the sheer newness of 3D printing technology makes it a fascinating opportunity and challenge. I love challenges that involve creating new things in unexpected ways.

Resources

3D Print Services
Shapeways - https://www.shapeways.com/
i.Materialise - https://i.materialise.com/
Sculpteo - http://www.sculpteo.com/en/
RedEye On Demand - http://www.redeyeondemand.com/
3D ProParts - http://www.3dproparts.com/

PinShape - https://www.pinshape.com/
3DLT - https://3dlt.com/
Threeding - https://www.threeding.com/

3D Model Depository
Ponoko Product Plans -
http://www.ponoko.com/showroom/product-plans/
Thingiverse - https://www.thingiverse.com/
CG Trader - http://www.cgtrader.com/
CNC King - http://cncking.com/3d-printer-projects.html
Yobi3D - http://yobi3d.com/#!/

Crowdsourcing 3D Printing
Makexyz - http://www.makexyz.com/
100K Garages - http://www.100kgarages.com/
KraftWurx - http://www.kraftwurx.com/
MakerFactory - http://makerfactory.com/
3D Hubs - http://3dhubs.com/

3D Printing News
3Ders - http://www.3ders.org/
Fabbaloo - http://www.fabbaloo.com/
3D Printing Industry - http://3dprintingindustry.com/
3D Print - http://3dprint.com/

3D Printers
RepRap - http://reprap.org/
Cubify - http://cubify.com/
MakerBot - http://www.makerbot.com/
Type A Machines - http://typeamachines.com/
Dremel 3D - http://3dprinter.dremel.com/

3D Modeling Software
Blender - http://www.blender.org/
MeshLab - http://meshlab.sourceforge.net/
SketchUp - http://sketchup.google.com/
123D Design - http://www.123dapp.com/
123Catch - http://www.123dapp.com/catch
3D Tin - http://www.3dtin.com/

Tinkercad - https://tinkercad.com/home/
AutoCAD - http://usa.autodesk.com/autocad-products/
Maya - http://www.autodesk.com/products/maya/overview
Rhino3D - http://www.rhino3d.com/
SolidWorks - http://www.solidworks.com/
ZBrush - http://www.pixologic.com/home.php

3D Printing Books
Fabricated: The New World of 3D Printing -
http://www.amazon.com/exec/obidos/ASIN/1118350634/fabbaloo-20/

Makers: The New Industrial Revolution -
http://www.amazon.com/gp/product/0307720950/ref=as_li_tf_tl?ie=U
TF8&camp=1789&creative=9325&creativeASIN=0307720950&linkCo
de=as2&tag=fabbaloo-20
Getting Started With MakerBot -
http://www.amazon.com/gp/product/1449338658/ref=as_li_tf_tl?ie=U
TF8&camp=1789&creative=9325&creativeASIN=1449338658&linkCo
de=as2&tag=fabbaloo-20
Rule 34 -
http://www.amazon.com/gp/product/1937007669/ref=as_li_tf_tl?ie=U
TF8&camp=1789&creative=9325&creativeASIN=1937007669&linkCo
de=as2&tag=fabbaloo-20
Practical 3D Printers: The Science and Art of 3D Printing -
http://www.amazon.com/gp/product/1430243929/ref=as_li_tf_tl?ie=U
TF8&camp=1789&creative=9325&creativeASIN=1430243929&linkCo
de=as2&tag=fabbaloo-20

Scanners and Scanning Services
123D Catch - http://123dapp.com/catch
Creaform - http://www.creaform3d.com/
Cubify Capture - http://www.cubify.com/products/capture/
DAVID-Laser Scanner - http://www.david-laserscanner.com/
NextEngine - http://www.nextengine.com/
ReconstructMe - http://reconstructme.net/
Skanect - http://skanect.manctl.com/
Makerbot Digitizer - https://store.makerbot.com/digitizer

Materials and Accesories

3DHacker - http://3dhacker.com/
Bucktown Polymers - http://bucktownpolymers.com/polymer00.html
Fabberworld - http://www.fabberworld.com/
Faberdashery - http://www.faberdashery.co.uk/
FormFutura - http://www.formfutura.com/
MakerBot - http://store.makerbot.com/
MakerGear -http://www.makergear.com/
Orbi-Tech -http://www.orbi-tech.de/shop/index.php
Plastic Webshop - http://www.plasticwebshop.com/
RepRapCentral - http://www.reprapcentral.com/
RepRapPro - http://reprappro.com/
RepRapSource - http://www.reprapsource.com/
Ultimachine - http://ultimachine.com/catalog

About the Author

Yoni Binstock is on a mission to use technology to create a more just and sustainable world.

He received his BA in Political Science from Rollins College, his MA in Energy and Environmental Analysis from Boston University. He then worked as the fifth employee at a tech startup in Cambridge for a year. Afterwards, he created a website called Climate Scores that graded Congressmen on climate change. In 2012, he worked at the nonprofit, Ashoka, managing their online fundraising strategy. After working there, he organized TEDxRosslyn, started a mobile app company, traveled Europe, and got married. In the past year, they moved to the Bay Area where he's worked at SolarMosaic, Solar City, and Change.org.

He's lived in Los Angeles, Cleveland, Orlando, Boston, Washington DC, Sydney, Tel Aviv, Chennai (India), and currently resides in San Francisco.

Yoni is now working on building his 3D printing empire and creating a Chrome extension that helps people disconnect from the internet called Goodnight Chrome.

When not talking in the third person, Yoni likes to read, run, and spend time with his wife.

Learn more about Yoni at www.yonibinstock.com and if you have any questions about 3D printing, don't hesitate at all to email him at ybinstock@gmail.com

Thank you

Thank you so much for purchasing and reading this book. You should now have the knowledge to start your own 3D Printing business.

Please Leave a Review

As an independent author, I rely on my readers to post positive reviews on Amazon. Your experience with my ebook is very important to me and I encourage you to share your thoughts for everyone to see.

Step 1: Go to Amazon and search for the book "How to Become a 3D Printing Entrepreneur"
Step 2: At the top there is a star rating along with the number of customer reviews. Click on "customer review".
Step 3: Click on "Create your own review" and follow the rest of Amazon's instructions. Your positive review would truly mean a lot to me.

Thank you and if for any reason you are not happy with your purchase, please send me an email at ybinstock at gmail dot com and I will send you a full refund.